AF265160

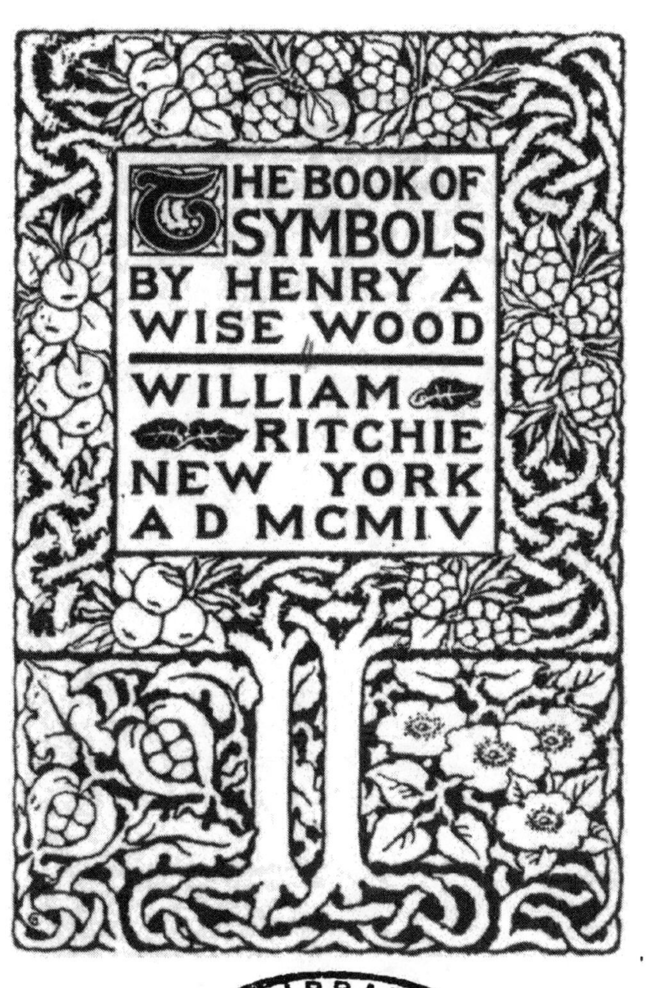

LIBRARY
OF THE
UNIVERSITY

Copyright, 1904,
by
Henry A. Wise Wood,
Entered at Stationers' Hall,
London.

Printed at Boston, U. S. A., by the Plimpton Press.

161125

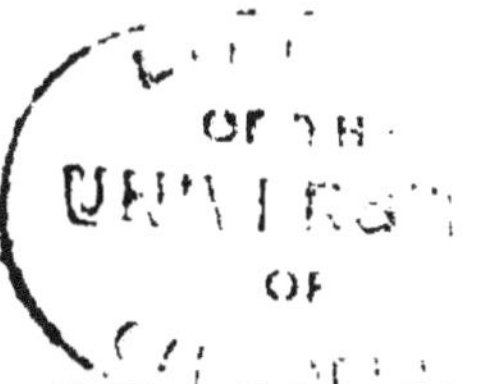

THE spell of ages settled on my
    dream,
And, through vague, haunting
    wraiths of Man's old hopes,
I saw his myriad temples, naked
    to the winds,
Whence came thin voices, cry-
    ing ceaselessly:
Insatiate Time, thou slayer of
    spent beliefs,
Where sit our Gods? — Where
    serve their worshipers?

OF THE
UNIVERSITY
OF

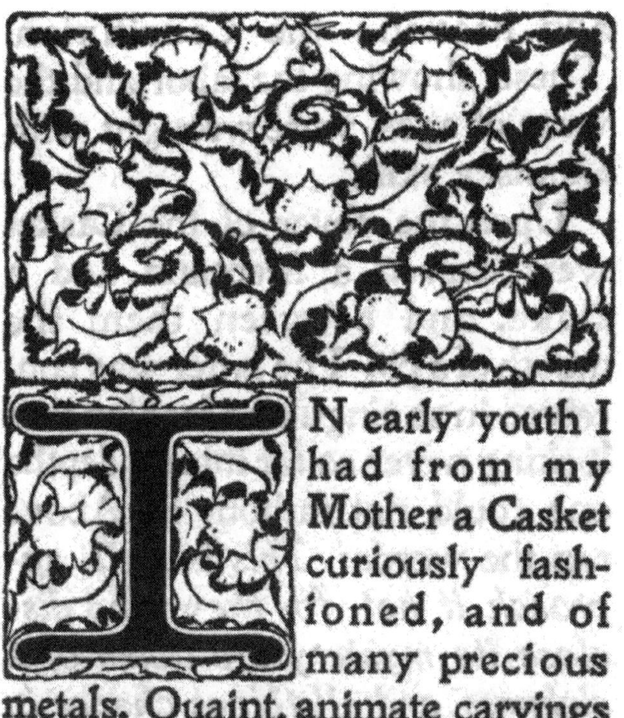

IN early youth I had from my Mother a Casket curiously fash-ioned, and of many precious metals. Quaint, animate carvings of ancient scenes were upon its sides: the Garden of Eden; an elaborate edifice which seemed to span the void between earth

and heaven; the Crucifixion.
These, showing the labor and the
wear of ages, were wrought with
exquisite skill.

Upon the cover of the Casket
were carven a firebrand and a
stake, and between them the
mouth of a pit. The latter was conceived in so singular a fashion that
looking never so far into its depths
one could not fathom it. Above
ran the words: *This is Hell, approach it not, for they who disclose its mystery are taken of a
sickness, and all things change in
their sight.* To me this inscription
seemed terrible; I dared not gaze
into the pit, and, when the box
rested with its cover uppermost, I

held my hand over it, for I was afraid.

Underneath, also, the box was of strange designing. Out of the center of the bottom peered an eye, like the sun, and from it rays shot to all of the corners of the Casket, and round about its sides, and upwardly over the edges of its top; while from all of the sides of the cover these rays gathered, and poured into the very mouth of hell.

Into the eye I feared to look, for over it, too, was an inscription that made me shrink in terror from its words: *The Eye of God sees, but it may not be seen; peer not into its depths,* nor attempt the mysteries within it, for he who reveals the Unknown shall be cast out of the haunts of men. The cruelty of the punishment shook me; I feared lest I might see, and so I ever held the box with its bottom from me. If, inadvertently, I should meet the eye, and penetrate its mysteries—how awful would be the cost!

So I bore the Casket close between my hands; the one above, the other beneath it. I would have hidden it, had I not been charged to bear it reverently, patiently, faithfully; or have wrapped it out of sight in the folds of my garments, had the scenes upon its

sides not held me so bound that
I could not withdraw myself from
the strange influences which they
wielded.

PON one panel it bore
a mystic nature scene:
a deep forest crowned
two rolling hills; be-
tween the hills a valley of luxuri-
ant undergrowth, part lighted,
part dark; and in the midst there-
of a clear, cool stream, with slop-
ing green borders of moss. Overhead, the outreaching branches
of the wood waved in the wind,

and in waving shook the long
strands of sunlight which kind-
led the many hues of the depths
beneath. Here, by the water,
half screened by the glistening
foliage of its brink, rested a man
and a woman; and as their voices
mingled with the r-u-u-l-l of the
brook, there came to me out of the
picture its transcendent meanings.

The woman and the man had
lived, wandered, and dreamed;
together they had come through
the lowlands, over the highlands,
into the forest; had seen the clouds
and the sea, the sunrise and the
noon, the sunset and the coming
of the stars; they had plucked the
flowers of the earth and trod the

gardens of the sky, and now they
had come by the brook and were
resting. They had seen all, and
it had wearied them.

The woman said: *How beautiful it is,*—and their eyes drank
the glories of the valley—*and how
peaceful.* The swirl of the water
made music of the thought, and
they listened.

Said the man: *How good is
the shade,*—the shafts of sunlight
sped afar off down the stream—
*and the solitude, how deep!*—the
sounds of the wood fell away—
*How soft the moss,*—the tendrils
of their couch pressed tiny fingers
to his side—*and how sweet is
the odor of your hair!*

The woman sighed. *It is all so beautiful, and you are a part of it, . . . and I am a part of it. I seem to see you, and yet to see with you; we are alike, yet unalike. You please me, as all else pleases me, and — the warmth of your body attracts me.*

Her words floated off; the woman and the man lay close together, and the breeze bore her hair across the intervening space. The clouds as they passed unnoticed overhead varied the shadows cast by her limbs upon the moss.

The man watched her; the dark background of the forest threw into relief the delicately modelled outlines of her form. Where the perception of companionship alone had reigned, there now stole in upon him a sense of something overlooked. The soft hues of the woman, the rhythm of the undulations of her body, the beauty of the hand that lay palm-uppermost between them—unfolding, like a lily upon the green surface of a lake—the glistening arm, the shoulder, the neck; the warmth and the fullness of life which they bespoke; these, all of these, stole in upon the man,—and he knew that there were secrets in the unopened volume of woman, which awaited but the turning of the title-page.

17

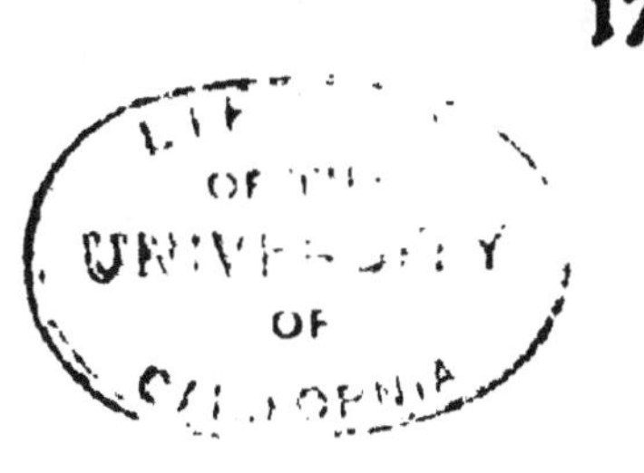

A tense, unbroken silence drew about them; the wood seemed to gather its children and stand afar off, the sky and its filmy cloud-forms faded into the realms of the unseen, the moist, soft bank upon which they lay passed from their senses, and the r-u-u-l-l of the stream as it swept from their hearing lent its throb to the flood that was coursing their veins.

The woman understood, and trembled, and the petals of her hand quivered in the green moss: the current of a new yearning had sprung within her; she felt it flood her lips, her throat, her breasts; felt it thrust aside the consciousness of all outward being, and,

18

thrilled with a supreme joy,timidly she awaited the moment of initial ecstacy.• And the brook sang a paean to Nature, as it wandered away to the sea.

This scene, I loved; and was never weary of looking at it. Nevertheless, it was evil, for an inscription called it the *Beginning of Evil*, and said: *Having peace, Man sought pleasure—and, finding pleasure, ne'er again had peace.*

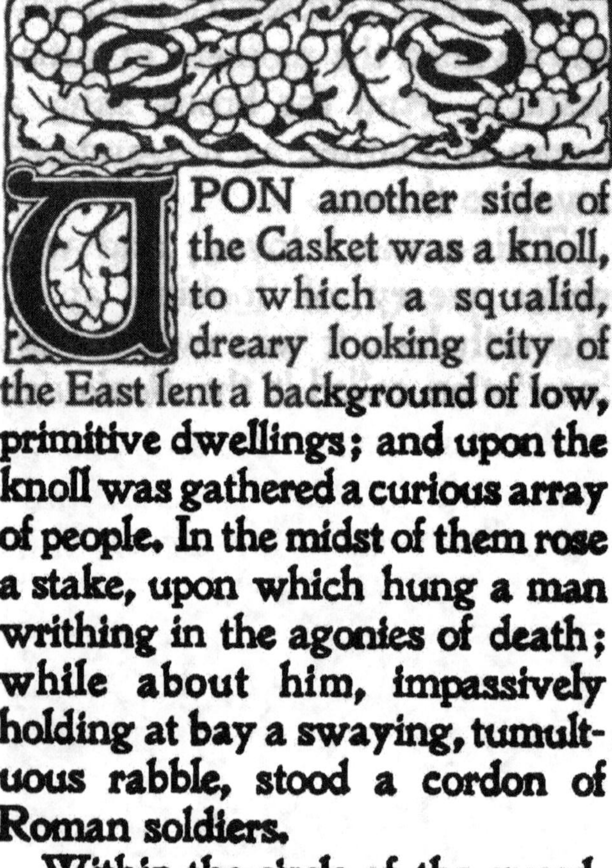

UPON another side of the Casket was a knoll, to which a squalid, dreary looking city of the East lent a background of low, primitive dwellings; and upon the knoll was gathered a curious array of people. In the midst of them rose a stake, upon which hung a man writhing in the agonies of death; while about him, impassively holding at bay a swaying, tumultuous rabble, stood a cordon of Roman soldiers.

Within the circle of the guard,

their faces strained and their eyes streaming, a group of men in anguish watched the sufferings of their leader, and at his feet, shaken with grief, there knelt a woman weeping.  Passing to and fro, intent upon their duties, stolidly moved those of the soldiery who were charged with the work of execution.

Over this scene there hung an atmosphere of suspense, accentuated by the cries of the throng, by the low-spoken words of the executioners, by the sobs of the woman, or by the moans of the now scarce struggling figure at the stake. As the laughter and jeers of the mob died away, and more distant sounds made themselves heard, the tension seemed to grow unendurable, and many of those who mutely watched turned from the sufferings they beheld. The baying of dogs in the town, the herd-cries from the hills round about, the routine noises from distant habitations, all these served to throw over the cruel spectacle a veil of utter commonplace, and to lend to the killing of this man, the world's gentle Egotist, an aspect of infinite dreariness.

The inscription of this picture I could neither clearly see, nor wholly understand; it was of strange characters, in part effaced,

but this much was I able to read:
*and he who would uplift, first
humbly must yield.*

This carving, my Mother had
said, was of the Atonement, an ex-
piation of the evil of the world, of
which the root was depicted upon
another side of the Casket. This
was not plain to me, but I accepted
it, and regarded the subject with
reverent awe, as a matter that was
not to be scrutinized, nor inquired
into. Nevertheless, like the altar-
lamp at a shrine, burned without
ceasing the question: *If beauty be
truth, and love be right, and to
live be good, why needed to be
atoned that which I had seen upon
an opposite panel of the box?*

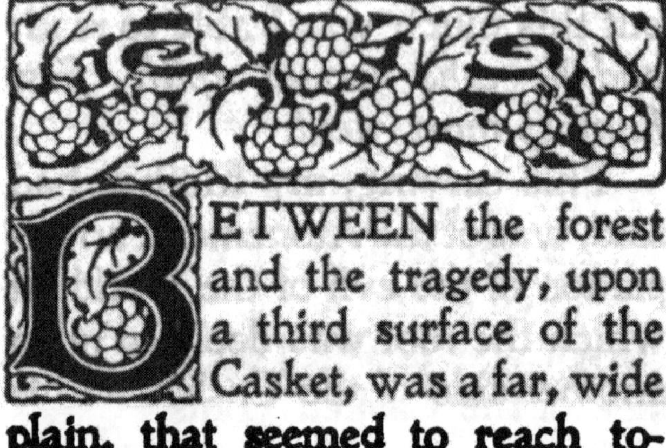

ETWEEN the forest and the tragedy, upon a third surface of the Casket, was a far, wide plain, that seemed to reach towards me from out the dusk of the very beginning of things human. Dotting its horizon were rude heaps of fallen stones, shattered temples of long-forgotten cults, whose blocks and pillars, scarce shapen by hand, were but dimly visible through the gray mists shrouding the plain upon which they lay.

Strewn hither and thither over its dim expanse, their cloisters fantastically interwoven, in the distance crude and timid in design, but ever as they neared me growing in power and beauty, pile succeeded to pile, structure to structure, bespeaking Faith's many culminations. Each seemed to have risen upon the ground of Man's necessity, and proudly in turn to have trumpeted the challenge: *I SHALL SATISFY!*

Among these ruins was every fashion of Man's art of building; in each he had expressed, as in him best it lay, his awe in the presence of the All-Mysterious. By thrusting toward the skies

with all his might his loftiest
deeds of beauty, he had sought
to do obeisance, and to propi-
tiate the dreaded Hand, which
he felt, but could not see.
Blood, treasure, and thought, fe-
verishly he had spent, and out of
his very abasement, springing
from his humility, and nurtured
while he lay prone upon earth,
one hand beating his breast, the
other timidly fashioning, blos-
somed and bloomed the exotic
which we call Art.

Forth from every portion of the
plain; from each fallen pile, from
structures shaken with Time's
ague, and from others of more
modern mould, the while I

26

watched, came spirits dumbly moving into line. Each bore, in hands, on back, or dragged behind with ropes, a brick, a stone, a pillar, to a spot where other spirits dumbly set these up, and builded, wide and high, in its thews a bit of every ancient fane, a towering edifice whose rising bastions cleft the mists, to shame the dazzling splendor of our noonday sun.

Round about this temple wailed the World, and lavished upon its altars blood, and gold, and thought; and daily the World slew itself that the crimson-bannered battlements might greet the sun full rich in Man's life-color, thus vaunting its God's debt to Man, for Man's self-sacrifice.

So ran the strange fancy wrought by this picture, which I had been taught to revere, to love, and to cleave to in hours of trouble. Its edifice had been called the *Rock upon which is founded all good; the World's refuge from evil,* and, within its archives only, I had been told, lay all of the past that bore worth for the future. Bent upon seeking asylum, many times had my spirit approached its open portals, but the sounds within — the clank of golden chains — had startled it, and each time wearily my spirit withdrew.

OF THE
UNIVERSITY

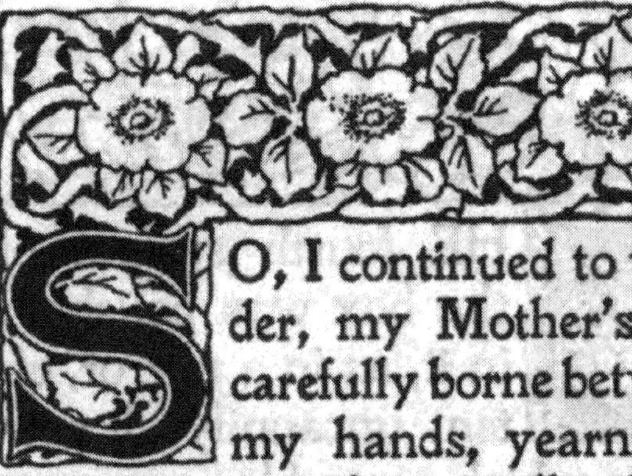

SO, I continued to wander, my Mother's gift carefully borne between my hands, yearningly looking upon the woodland picture, notwithstanding I had been taught that it was the root of all pain.

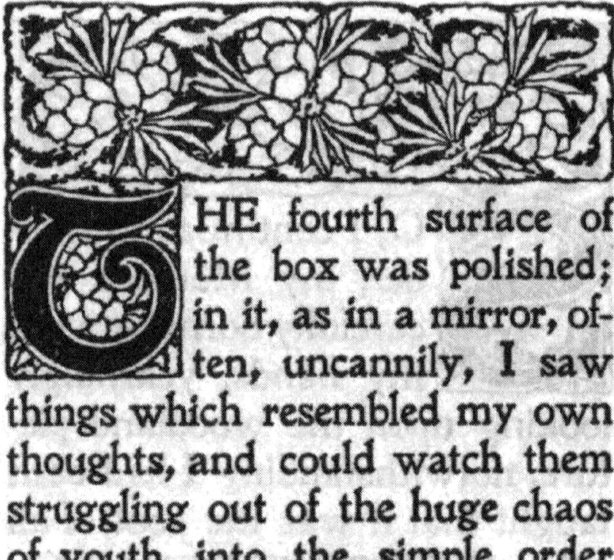

THE fourth surface of the box was polished; in it, as in a mirror, often, uncannily, I saw things which resembled my own thoughts, and could watch them struggling out of the huge chaos of youth, into the simple order of maturity.

This side of the Casket unceasingly held me in its magic spell, and the transformations which it reflected blenched me at times with horror. In its mysterious depths I could see a  cold finger

touch, one after another, things
long held dear to my heart and
passionately cherished by me ;
things which, at its approach,
drooped or vanished, or, suddenly
sprang into new shape, and took
their places as mere elements in
the tremendous hypothesis which
was forming within me—forming
at the cost of such heavy travail.

Loved conceptions would be-
come misconceptions, while in-
herited beliefs, affectionately nurtured, fled at the chill touch of
that inexorable finger. Heartsick
and weary, with all my soul's
strength, often I prayed to possess
once again youth's sunlit, trustful

hours, and its mother-taught,
safe-guarding formulas; and, fi-
nally, one day, I thrust from me
the haunting mirror with its phan-
tom hand!

But the finger drew me back
to the dread phantasmagoria; I
could not escape it; the threads
of the hypothesis must be spun,
each must take its place, and, al-
though it serve as shroud to, the
dearest heart-held belief that lay
hidden in my breast, the fabric
must be fully woven. Then, weak
with dread, again I looked, and,
lo! it was finished; the hypothesis was formed, and it lay be-
fore me complete in every element.
The phantasms had fled, and in

their stead was a sweep of tran-
quil sky; my travail was spent,
and, freed by the magic touch of
thought from the puny thraldom
of a Plan, in the clear light of the
Indisputable — which men call
Truth — I saw, with a fierce joy,
fierce as the joy of battle, which
is sweeter than all youth's ecsta-
cies, *Nature, the Juggernaut, un-
hasting, unthinking, heedlessly
onward-rolling upon its inexorable mission of consequence.*

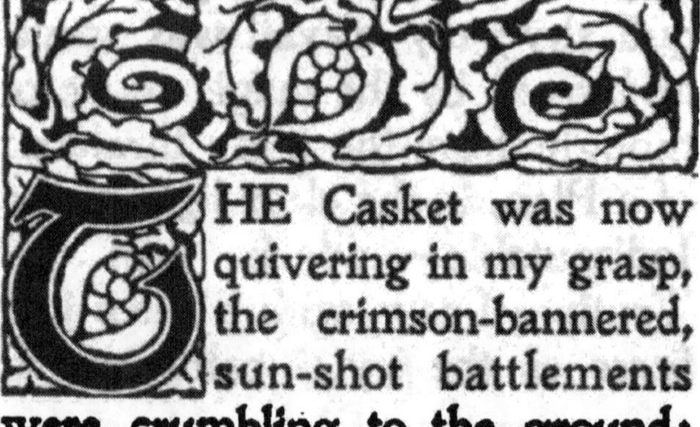

THE Casket was now quivering in my grasp, the crimson-bannered, sun-shot battlements were crumbling to the ground; the Castle of Fear had fallen, and, as through a golden mist, up from its shattered corridors arose the wondrous arts of Color, Form, and Sound, the World's inheritance, its richest legacies of Faith. The scene of the Crucifixion had vanished—in vain had the twin spirits Ignorance and Intolerance striven to quench in the hearts of

men the spark out of which
Thought and Compassion were
summoning the love of kind—and
in its stead stood there the spirit
of Eternal Kindness, saying:
*Condemn not, lest the flames of
resentment consume the vessel in
which they burn. Ye cannot reach
the ancestry of this day's mis-
deeds, but the morrow's worth
waits upon its inheritance—
therefore, garner ye all good.*

Then, with a wrench, as if it
were being torn from me by all
of the hands of Time, the Casket
leapt from my grasp, and lay at
my feet, open. The ground trembled and rocked, as if in the throes
of convulsion, and out of the Cas-

ket there sprang a **Man**, facing the level rays of the new-day's sun, firm-eyed and strong, one hand aloft to command his fate, while with the other he thrust back to their graves the grim hordes of the past, hugging their implements of terror, worship, and propitiation.

And up from their knees to **Man's** full height rose other men, stripping from death its hideous jest of life, and gazing with fearless eyes into the sun. Unawed by the menace of the Universe, these grasped the earth and bent it to their need; wrung from its tardy lips new, frank, replies, and conjured from every firmamental star its seething tribute to **Man's** master mind.

From its slumber of untold cen-
turies the World seemed suddenly
to have waked, and at a bound
to have passed from beneath the
sombre clouds of savagery, bar-
barism, and civilization, out into
the clear dawn of the god-un-
needing age of enlightenment.

37

LIBRARY
OF T
UNIVE
OF
CALIFORNIA

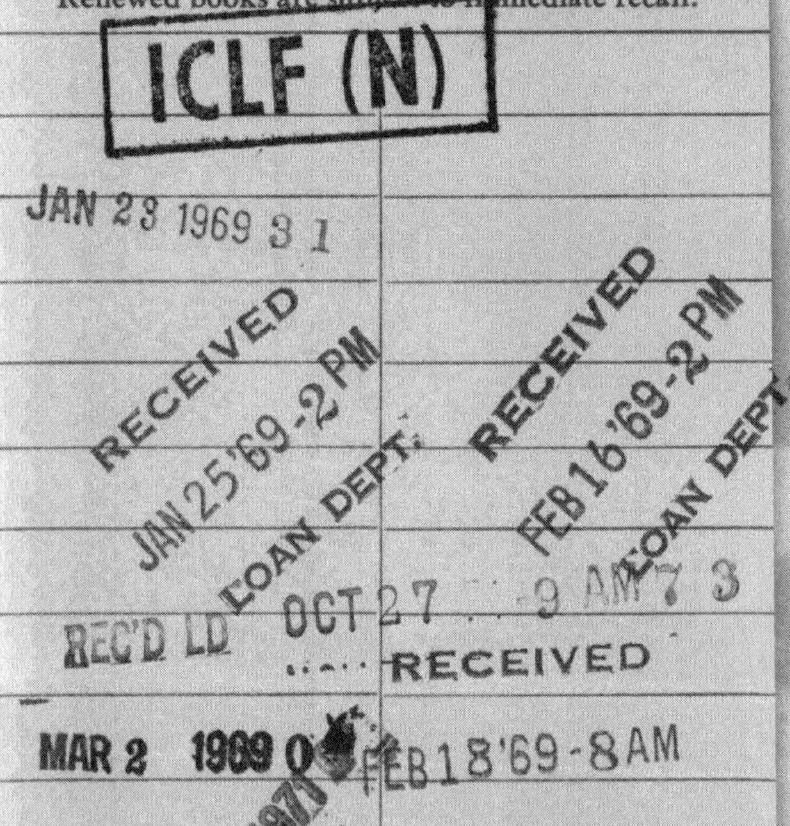
14 DAY USE
RETURN TO DESK FROM WHICH BORROWED
LOAN DEPT.
RENEWALS ONLY—TEL. NO. 642-3405
This book is due on the last date stamped below, or
on the date to which renewed.
Renewed books are subject to immediate recall.
ICLF (N)
JAN 23 1969 3 1
RECEIVED
JAN 25'69 -2 PM
LOAN DEPT.
RECEIVED
FEB 16 '69 -2 PM
LOAN DEPT.
REC'D LD
OCT 27 ... 9 AM 7 3
RECEIVED
MAR 2 1969 0
FEB 18 '69 -8 AM
NOV 10 1970
LOAN DEPT.

www.ingramcontent.com/pod-product-compliance
Lightning Source LLC
Chambersburg PA
CBHW061103050726
47592CB00004B/1805